TH

STEN

MACHINE CARBINE

FULLY ILLUSTRATED

The Naval & Military Press Ltd

Published by the
The Naval & Military Press
in association with the Royal Armouries

Unit 10 Ridgewood Industrial Park,
Uckfield, East Sussex, TN22 5QE
Tel: +44 (0) 1825 749494
Fax: +44 (0) 1825 765701

MILITARY HISTORY AT YOUR FINGERTIPS
www.naval-military-press.com

ONLINE GENEALOGY RESEARCH
www.military-genealogy.com

ONLINE MILITARY CARTOGRAPHY
www.militarymaproom.com

ROYAL
ARMOURIES

The Library & Archives Department at the
Royal Armouries Museum, Leeds, specialises
in the history and development of armour
and weapons from earliest times to the
present day. Material relating to the
development of artillery and modern
fortifications is held at the Royal
Armouries Museum, Fort Nelson.

For further information contact:
Royal Armouries Museum, Library, Armouries Drive,
Leeds, West Yorkshire LS10 1LT
Royal Armouries, Library, Fort Nelson, Down End Road, Fareham PO17 6AN

Or visit the Museum's website at
www.armouries.org.uk

*In reprinting in facsimile from the original, any imperfections are inevitably reproduced
and the quality may fall short of modern type and cartographic standards.*

Printed and bound by CPI Antony Rowe, Eastbourne

CONTENTS

THE
STEN MACHINE CARBINE

DATA

GUN

Overall length of carbine with butt	...	...	$29\frac{1}{2}$ in.
Overall length of carbine without butt	...	...	19 in.
Weight (without magazine)	...	...	$6\frac{1}{2}$ lb.
Weight with magazine (unloaded)	...	...	$7\frac{1}{4}$ lb.
Weight with magazine (loaded) ...	...	...	8 lb.
Length of barrel	...	...	$7\frac{1}{2}$ in.
Length of barrel nut	...	...	$2\frac{3}{4}$ in.
Length of breech block	...	...	$5\frac{3}{4}$ in.
Weight of breech block	...	...	$1\frac{1}{4}$ lb.

MAGAZINE

Box type capacity	...	...	32 rds.
Box type weight, fully loaded	...	...	$1\frac{1}{4}$ lb.
Magazine filler, weight ...	...	...	5 oz.

AMMUNITION

9 millimetres.

The gun is capable of firing most makes of 9-mm. ammunition, British, American, German and Italian.

SIGHTS

Foresight is triangular in shape.

Backsight is of the fixed aperture type.

These sights are used when firing from the shoulder and are reasonably accurate up to 100 yards.

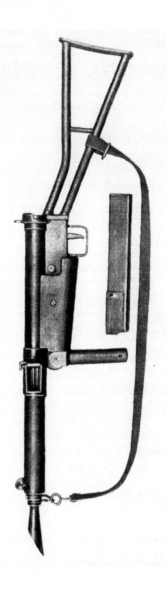

THE STEN MACHINE CARBINE MARK I

GENERAL DESCRIPTION

The Sten Machine Carbine is a small and compact automatic weapon, it is a British invention, and can be likened to the Thompson Machine Carbine in many respects.

It has, however, neither the finish nor the complicated mechanism of the Thompson Machine Carbine.

It is simple to produce, there is little about it that can go wrong, and it is very simple in operation. In spite of this, it is very hardy and will stand up to a good deal of rough usage.

A change lever is incorporated in the mechanism, permitting the carbine to be fired in single shots or in bursts of fire.

There is no cooling device on this weapon, but it is capable of firing from between eight and ten magazines in continuous bursts before getting too hot to hold. At this stage, dipping in water will effect the necessary cooling.

The Mark I or Mark II model can be packed in a very small space by the removal of the butt and barrel and the rotation of the magazine housing to a downward position.

The carbine is of the blow-back type; thus when a round is fired the breech block is forced to the rear position by a portion of the explosive force.

An interesting feature of this weapon is its fixed firing pin.

THE STEN MACHINE CARBINE MARK II

MECHANISM

FORWARD ACTION (change lever set for single shots)

Cock carbine.

To fire the carbine single shots it is first necessary to push the end of the change lever marked " R " in towards the body of the carbine.

On the trigger being pressed, the sear is disengaged from the bent on the underside of the breech block. The compressed return spring pushes the breech block forward, and the bent comes in contact with the tripping lever, forcing it downwards; this action allows the sear to resume its original position.

The forward movement of the breech block continues until the two forward ends of the ribs forming the ejection way on the breech block come into contact with the base of the topmost round in the magazine; this action pushes the round from the magazine to the chamber. At this point the extractor engages in the groove at the base of the cartridge case. The fixed firing pin now strikes the cartridge cap, exploding the charge.

BACKWARD ACTION

A portion of the explosive force drives the breech block rearwards. As this action takes place the empty case is held on the face of the breech block by the extractor.

The ejector, which protrudes into the body of the gun, strikes the empty case, ejecting it through the ejection port situated on the right side of the carbine. The breech block continues its backward movement, compressing the return spring, until the bent engages with the sear, when the mechanism is held in the rear position until the trigger is again pressed.

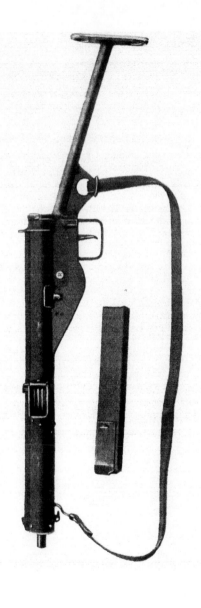

THE STEN MACHINE CARBINE MARK III

BACKWARD AND FORWARD ACTION (change lever set for automatic firing)

To set the gun to fire automatically it will be necessary to push the end of the change lever marked " A " towards the body of the carbine.

The effect of this is to push the tripping lever out of the path of the bent on the underside of the breech block.

The mechanism therefore is similar to single-shot firing, except that there is no tripping-lever action; this permits the sear to remain depressed and allows the carbine to continue firing as long as the trigger is pressed and there are rounds in the magazine.

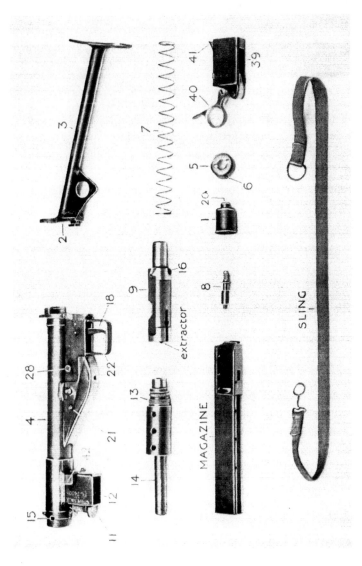

3

7

41

40

39

5

6

1

2

9

16

extractor

8

28

18

22

4

13

21

42

14

12

15

11

MAGAZINE

SLING

STRIPPING

No attempt must be made to strip the carbine until an inspection has been made to ensure that it is safe to do so. After this inspection leave the breech block in its forward position, and ensure that there is no magazine in the carbine.

BUTT

With the thumb of the right hand press in the rounded end of the return spring housing (1), disengaging it from the butt plate (2); at the same time slide the butt (3) in a downward direction clear of the body (4).

BODY GROUP

(i) *Return Spring Cap, Housing and Return Spring.*—Using the thumb and finger of the right hand, press in the return spring cap (5) about a quarter of an inch, rotating in an anti-clockwise direction, thus releasing the two small lugs (6) on the cap from their recesses in the body of the carbine. As the lugs clear the recesses, pressure will be felt on the return spring cap and housing. This is caused by the pressure of the return spring (7). Control this pressure and remove the return spring cap, housing and return spring.

(ii) *Cocking Handle and Breech Block.*—Using the cocking handle (8), withdraw the breech block (9) rearward until the cocking handle is in line with the safety slot (10). The cocking handle must now be rotated about half-way into the safety slot; this permits the withdrawal of the cocking handle. Slide the breech block out of the body.

(iii) *Barrel (Mark II pattern).*—The plunger (11), which is situated on the side of the magazine housing (12), should now be disengaged by pulling outwards. At the same time, the magazine housing should be rotated anti-clockwise to a position under the body of the carbine. The barrel locking nut (13) can now be unscrewed and the barrel (14) and locking nut removed together.

NOTE.

(i) It is strongly recommended that no further stripping of this
weapon should be permitted. The stripping detailed above
is considered to be sufficient to teach the man the working
of the carbine and also covers the stripping necessary for
care and cleaning.

(ii) In the Mark III model it is not possible to remove the
barrel, as it is surrounded by a casing which is itself a
fixture.

ASSEMBLING

BARREL

The barrel and locking nut will be assembled together.
Place the rear portion of the barrel into the front end of the
body, making sure that it is fully home.

Screw up barrel locking nut until it is hand tight.

Turn the magazine housing in a clockwise direction, when the
plunger will re-engage in the hole (15) in front of the body.

In assembling, it will be noted that either numbers or a line are
inscribed on the barrel. When assembled, these numbers or line
should be in rough alignment with the foresight.

BREECH BLOCK AND COCKING HANDLE

Slide the breech block into the body, taking care that the cocking handle hole (16) in the breech block is in alignment with the
cocking handle slot (17). During this action the trigger (18)
must be kept pressed so that the sear (19) does not prevent the
forward movement of the breech block by protruding into the
body of the carbine.

Push the breech block forward until the cocking handle hole is
opposite the safety slot (10).

Insert the cocking handle into the breech block, and, retaining
pressure on the trigger, push the breech block fully forward.

NOTE.—Do not drop the breech block into the body, as this
may cause damage to the ejector.

RETURN SPRING, HOUSING AND CAP

Insert the return spring into the body of the carbine, place the return spring housing over the end of the return spring and the return spring cap over the stud (20) on the end of the return spring housing.

Align the two lugs (6) on the cap with the recesses in the body, and press forward so that the projections enter the recesses. When clear, turn the cap about a quarter of an inch in a clockwise direction.

BUTT

Using the top front face of the butt, press in the stud on the return spring housing and slide the butt upwards until engaged.

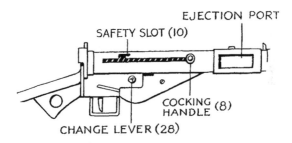

RIGHT-HAND SIDE OF BODY (MARK II)

TRIGGER
MECHANISM
COVER

washers

ADDITIONAL STRIPPING

The stripping described here is not meant for the man to practise, but it is felt that some guidance should be given to those charged with the repair or the changing of broken parts of this weapon.

TRIGGER MECHANISM

(i) *Trigger Mechanism Cover.*—Remove the two screws (21) from the triangular-shaped mechanism cover. These screws are situated about two inches in front of the trigger guard (22), one on each side of the cover. The cover can now be pulled off.

NOTE.—The screws mentioned above are not present in the Mark II model; in this type the casing is sprung on.

(ii) *Trigger Spring.*—Unhook the trigger spring (23) from the tripping-lever pawl (24) and from the trigger.

(iii) *Tripping-lever Pawl.*—Rotate the tripping-lever pawl to an upright position and remove it from the lower portion of the sear.

(iv) *Sear.*—Remove the sear axis pin (25) and raise the sear out of the carbine. To do this it will be necessary to raise the tripping lever (26) to allow the sear to come out.

(v) *Change Lever.*—Withdraw the split pin (27) from the change lever (28), raise the tripping lever clear of the recess (29) in the change lever, and remove it.

(vi) *Trigger Axis Pin.*—Remove the trigger axis pin (30). This looks like a piece of bent wire and is situated on the right side of the carbine just above the trigger guard.

(vii) *Tripping Lever and Trigger.*—Withdraw the tripping lever and trigger in a forward direction from the trigger group. To separate the trigger from the tripping lever, remove the axis pin.

ASSEMBLY OF TRIGGER MECHANISM

All parts should be assembled in the order they are shown here.

(i) *Trigger and Tripping Lever.*

(*a*) To assemble trigger and tripping lever, hold trigger with trigger spring hook pointing to the left, place tripping lever in slot in top of the trigger, ensuring that raised portion of tripping lever is uppermost. Replace axis pin.

(*b*) To replace trigger and tripping lever in carbine, hold tripping lever, with raised portion pointing forward. The trigger spring hook should now be pointing to the rear. Lower trigger into body, and push backward on tripping lever. This will have the effect of placing trigger correctly in the trigger guard. Replace trigger axis pin.

(ii) *Change Lever.*—This is replaced through the large hole in the left of the body of the carbine (carbine upside down). It will be necessary to raise the tripping lever slightly to allow this. The plungers (31) on the end of the change lever should engage with the body. Replace the split pin, splaying it flush with the change lever.

(iii) *Sear.*—Raise the tripping lever sufficiently to allow the insertion of the sear in the body. Placing the tripping lever under the arm on the lower portion of the sear, with the nose of the sear pointing rearward, lower sear into body and replace axis pin.

(iv) *Tripping-lever Pawl.*—Replace the tripping-lever pawl on the arm (32) attached to the lower portion of the sear. This is done by holding the pawl with the hook portion pointing upwards and forwards, sliding it on the arm. The long arm of the pawl (33) should now be resting on the tripping lever.

(v) *Trigger Spring.*—Replace the trigger spring by hooking one end to the hook on the trigger and the other to the hook on the tripping-lever pawl.

(vi) *Trigger Mechanism Cover.*—Replace the trigger mechanism cover and screw in the two screws, care being taken to replace the washers before inserting the screws.

16

MAGAZINE

This is the box type, consisting of the following parts: —

- (i) Casing (34).
- (ii) Platform (35).
- (iii) Spring (36).
- (iv) Bottom plate (37).
- (v) Retainer plate and stud (38).

It will be necessary, on occasions, to strip the magazine for cleaning. This should not be done more than is absolutely necessary, as continual stripping is liable to make the magazine unserviceable.

STRIPPING MAGAZINE

Disengage the stud on the retaining plate from the bottom plate by pushing inwards. Slide off the bottom plate; care must be taken to prevent the spring flying out. Withdraw the spring and platform.

ASSEMBLING OF MAGAZINE

Guide the platform and spring into the casing. Compress the spring by exerting pressure on the retaining plate. Slide the bottom plate into position. The stud on the retaining plate should reposition itself in the hole in the bottom plate. Should it not do so, a tap with the hand is all that will be necessary.

MAGAZINE FILLER

There are two types of filler in use with this weapon. They are similar in design, the difference being in the position of the spring catch. The filler consists of the following parts: —

- (i) Casing (39).
- (ii) Brass lever (40).
- (iii) Spring catch (41).

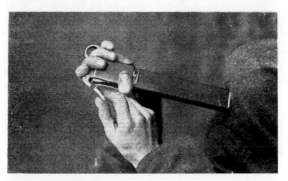

MAGAZINE FILLING

The greatest care must be taken to ensure that both magazines and rounds are clean before commencing to fill.

It is also necessary to count the rounds as they are placed in the magazine; the magazine will hold 32 rounds.

Owing to the powerful magazine spring, filling by hand (similar to the filling of the Thompson Machine Carbine) is a very slow process; therefore a filler is provided to give quick filling.

TO FILL THE MAGAZINE

Slide the casing of the filler on to the top of the magazine, making certain that the spring catch engages.

Place the bottom plate of the magazine against the waist belt or any suitable place which will give steadiness to the magazine during the filling operations.

The left hand should now be placed on the brass lever, third finger through the ring, forefinger on the part where the lever joins the filler casing, second finger between ring and forefinger, with the little finger immediately behind the ring.

Press the back of the lever downwards; this depresses the magazine platform. Take some rounds in the right hand and place one round in under the brass lever, base first. Raise the lever, the hook portion of which will draw the round in under the lips. Press the lever down again, when the round will be correctly filled, and space left for the insertion of the next round to be filled. Continue this action for each round until the magazine is filled or the required number of rounds have been filled. A full motion of the lever in both directions must be made, otherwise faulty feeding may result. Remove the filler by pressing the spring catch away from the filler, sliding the filler clear of the magazine.

TO EMPTY THE MAGAZINE

The rounds can be removed from the magazine by pressing the base of the round forward, steadying its removal by the aid of the forefinger.

LOADING AND UNLOADING THE CARBINE

LOADING

Hold the carbine in the right hand, butt under the arm, fore-finger clear of the trigger, muzzle pointing downwards to an angle of about 45°.

Take the magazine in the left hand, nose of rounds pointing forward; slide the magazine into the magazine housing. Force is not necessary, but care should be exercised to ensure that the magazine is properly engaged.

The loading is completed by pulling the cocking handle to the rear position and moving it into the safety slot in the top of the body. Once it is realized that firing is likely, the cocking handle should be moved from the safety slot.

NOTE.

(*a*) Owing to the heavy weight of the breech block, and the light spring, care must be taken not to give the carbine a severe jolt, as this may cause the weapon to fire.

(*b*) If passing the carbine from one person to another, when it is loaded, but not cocked, great care must be taken that the cocking handle does not get caught up in clothing, equipment, etc., as this might be sufficient to cause the weapon to fire.

UNLOADING

Holding the weapon, as for "Loading," press the catch (42) on the magazine housing, in a downward direction, with the thumb of the left hand, withdrawing the magazine from its housing.

If not already cocked, pull the cocking handle back, holding the cocking handle with the left hand. Press the trigger, allowing the mechanism to go forward gently under control. In the interests of safety this action should be repeated.

THE SHOULDER POSITION

AIMING AND FIRING

AIMING

The sights fitted to this carbine are: foresight, triangular in shape, and a fixed aperture battle sight, sighted for use up to 100 yards.

The following rules should be observed when firing from the shoulder using sights:—

(i) Keep the sights upright.

(ii) Get the eye as close to the aperture as possible.

(iii) Look through the aperture and align the top of the foresight in the centre of the target.

FIRING

Insert fully loaded magazine in carbine. Pull back cocking handle to its fullest extent.

To fire single shots push the end of the change lever marked "R" in towards the body of the carbine (ensuring that the cocking handle is not in its safety slot). The carbine will now fire each time the trigger is pressed.

To fire bursts push the end of the change lever marked "A" in towards the body of the carbine (ensure that the cocking handle is not in its safety slot). The carbine will now fire in bursts, the length of burst depending on the length of time the trigger is pressed.

With practice it will be found possible to fire single shots with the carbine set for bursts.

It is recommended that the length of a burst should not exceed 3 rounds.

Observation of fire must be of a high standard if successful results are to be achieved.

Owing to the high rate of fire and the necessity for conserving ammunition, single-shot firing should be considered the normal method, and bursts to be used only in an emergency.

THE WAIST POSITION

FIRING POSITIONS

With a weapon of this type, the importance of adopting the correct position cannot be over-emphasized if the utmost fire effect is to be obtained.

Fire effect can only be obtained if the following three points are applied : —

(a) An aggressive attitude.

(b) Determination.

(c) Concentration on the target.

There are two positions for firing, and they are here described with the firer at the halt, which is the best way to fire. The weapon, however, can be fired when on the move.

THE SHOULDER POSITION

The butt is brought into the shoulder with the right hand gripping the butt firmly, forefinger on the trigger; the left hand is gripping the barrel nut with the hand under the magazine, little finger clear of the ejection opening. It is important that the grip is firmly maintained during the firing or inaccurate shooting will result.

The right elbow is raised, with the right shoulder pushed forward slightly.

The left leg should be advanced, with the knee bent and the right leg braced.

THE WAIST POSITION

The butt is placed at the waist, between the body of the firer and his right forearm; the hands are gripping as for the shoulder position.

The legs are in the same position as described in the shoulder position.

The alignment of the weapon on the target is greatly facilitated by pulling the left elbow close into the body.

IMMEDIATE ACTION

This carbine has very few stoppages, and when one does occur the immediate action explained here will remedy this at once. The main causes of stoppages are:

    (a) Empty magazine.

    (b) Fault in feed. This is caused by a second round rising from the magazine and obstructing the breech block on its way to the chamber to fire the first round.

    (c) Faulty ejection. The empty case is not properly ejected, remaining in the body of the carbine. This again obstructs the breech block.

    (d) Misfire. This may be due to a fault in the cartridge itself or to an accumulation of dirt on the face of the breech block, thus preventing the striker penetrating the cap.

The following immediate action will remedy the above:

    (i) If the stoppage is due to an empty magazine, change the magazine, cock the carbine and continue firing.

    (ii) If the stoppage is not due to an empty magazine, cock the carbine and inspect the ejection opening.

        (a) If no obstruction, continue to fire.

        (b) If there is an obstruction, shake it out and continue firing.

        (c) If the obstruction is a live round in the chamber and it cannot be shaken out, remove the magazine and fire it. Replace the magazine and continue to fire.

        (d) If the live round is a misfire it must be shaken out.

An additional cause of the carbine stopping is a burst case. This is of rare occurrence and is caused by excessive dirt in the chamber, or an obstruction preventing the complete entry of the cartridge into the chamber. The striker may thus fire the round when it is not completely in the chamber, giving a burst or separated case.

The immediate action described above will remedy these stoppages. The following additional points must be borne in mind:

(a) All portions of the burst case must be removed before firing is resumed.

(b) Examine the barrel; the bullet may still be in there.

(c) Should this stoppage recur, examine the breech block for excessive dirt and the chamber for burrs.

CLEANING

Strip the carbine as previously explained under the heading " Stripping."

The rifle pullthrough and flannelette are used for the cleaning of the barrel; the size of the flannelette should be 4 inches by 3 inches.

A gauze is provided, but should be used only when absolutely necessary.

The reoiling of the barrel is done by using flannelette size 4 inches by 2 inches.

The chamber can be cleaned and oiled using a piece of wood with a slot in the end, into which is inserted a piece of flannelette.

The remaining parts can be cleaned and oiled using clean and oily pieces of rag.

At all times the greatest attention must be given to the cleaning of the following parts:—

(a) Face of the breech block.

(b) The chamber.

(c) Inside the body of the gun.

(d) The ejector.

CLEANING BEFORE FIRING

It is of the utmost importance that the following points are attended to : —

Before firing, the carbine will be stripped as already explained, and *all trace of oil removed* and the carbine reassembled in this dry condition.

This weapon is constructed to fire without oil, and no firing should take place unless all oil has been removed.